Character Education

Peacefulness

by Lucia Raatma

Consultant:
Madonna Murphy, Ph.D.
Associate Professor of Education
University of St. Francis, Joliet, Illinois
Author, *Character Education in America's
Blue Ribbon Schools*

Bridgestone Books
an imprint of Capstone Press
Mankato, Minnesota

Bridgestone Books are published by Capstone Press
151 Good Counsel Drive, P.O. Box 669, Mankato, Minnesota 56002
http://www.capstone-press.com

Library of Congress Cataloging-in-Publication Data
Raatma, Lucia.
    Peacefulness/by Lucia Raatma.
    p. cm.—(Character education)
    Includes bibliographical references (p. 24) and index.
    Summary: Describes peacefulness as a virtue and suggests ways in which
children can recognize and practice it.
    ISBN 0-7368-0370-X
    1. Conduct of life—Juvenile literature. 2. Conflict management—Juvenile
relations. 3. Interpersonal conflict—Juvenile literature. [1. Conflict
management.] I. Title. II. Series.
BJ1595.R17 2000
179′.9—dc21
                                                                        99-29181
                                                                        CIP

Editorial Credits

Damian Koshnick, editor; Heather Kindseth, cover designer and illustrator;
    Kimberly Danger, photo researcher

Photo Credits

Mike Smith/FPG International LLC, 18
Norvia Behling, 6
Palma Allen, 10
Photo Network/Myrleen Ferguson Cate, cover, 4, 20
Unicorn Stock Photos/Eric R. Berndt, 16
Uniphoto, 12, 14; bachmann, 8

2 3 4 5 6 06 05 04 03 02 01

Table of Contents

Peacefulness

Peacefulness comes from a sense of calm within yourself. Peaceful people treat others with kindness. They solve problems by cooperating and talking with others. Peaceful people find good things in their everyday lives.

cooperate
to work with others;
to work together

Being Peaceful

Peacefulness is liking who you are. Being peaceful means you are calm and happy inside. You know that you cannot control what others do. People sometimes might make fun of you. But their words will not hurt you if you are happy with yourself.

Peacefulness with Family

Peacefulness is appreciating your family. Peacefulness means getting along with your brothers and sisters. It means laughing and talking with your parents. Peacefulness is sharing important moments with your family.

appreciate
to enjoy or value
something or someone

Peacefulness with Friends

People sometimes forget the score in a game. While playing baseball, you may think the score is 3 to 2. Friends on the other team might think it is 3 to 3. A peaceful solution would be to agree with them. Arguing about the score is not as fun as playing with friends.

solution

the answer to a problem

Peacefulness through Exercise

Daily activity can help you feel a sense of peacefulness. You need exercise to keep your body and mind healthy. Running, walking, and playing are good ways to exercise. Exercise can make you feel good.

Peacefulness at School

Peacefulness means working together. At school, you may want to do a project your way. Your classmate may have a different idea. Peacefulness means compromising. You can put your ideas together to make a new idea.

compromise
to agree to something that is
not exactly what you wanted

Please
Keep YOUR
Parks Clean.

Peacefulness in Your Community

Peacefulness comes from knowing you are safe. Peaceful communities have safe parks to visit. It is important to keep parks clean for everyone. A community is peaceful when people watch out for one another.

"I have a dream that my four children will one day live in a nation where they will not be judged by the color of their skin but by the content of their character."–Martin Luther King, Jr.

Peace and Martin Luther King, Jr.

Martin Luther King, Jr. was a civil rights leader in the 1960s. Martin worked so that people of all races would be treated equally. He fought against racism in a peaceful way. Martin gave speeches. He organized peaceful marches and sit-ins.

racism
to treat people unfairly
based on their race

Peacefulness and You

Peacefulness comes from accepting yourself and others. Peacefulness is about sharing ideas and helping other people. Peacefulness comes from inside. You are happy when you are peaceful.

Hands On: Peacefulness in the Newspaper

Peacefulness and fighting happen every day around the world. You can read about many of these events in the newspaper.

What You Need

An adult
A newspaper
Scissors

What You Do

1. Look through the newspaper with an adult each day for a week.
2. Ask the adult to help you find articles that tell about anger and fighting. Look for articles about peacefulness too.
3. Ask an adult to cut out the stories that you find.
4. Talk with your teacher and classmates about the news you found.

Talk about how the fighting could have been solved peacefully. Talk about what makes the peaceful stories good.

Words to Know

civil rights (SIV-il RITES)—the rights that all people have to freedom and equal treatment under the law

compromise (KOM-pruh-mize)—to agree to something that is not exactly what you wanted

cooperate (koh-OP-uh-rate)—to work with others; to work together.

racism (RAY-sism)—to treat people unfairly based on their race

sit-in (SIT-IN)—a peaceful act in which a group of people sit in a place or building to show their beliefs; Martin Luther King, Jr., organized sit-ins against racism.

Read More

Aber, Linda Williams. *101 Activities for Siblings Who Squabble: Projects and Games to Entertain and Keep the Peace.* New York: St. Martin's Griffin, 1995.

Bray, Rosemary L. *Martin Luther King.* New York: Greenwillow Books, 1995.

Schaefer, Lola M. *Martin Luther King, Jr.* Famous Americans. Mankato, Minn.: Pebble Books, 1999.

Internet Sites

Adventures from the Book of Virtues Home Page
http://www.pbs.org/adventures
The King Center
http://www.thekingcenter.com
We Can Work It Out Together
http://members.aol.com/pforpeace/WorkItOut

Index